HOW TO DEVELOP E.Q. FOR COMPETITIVE EXAMS

(JEE,NEET,CUET,ICAR,JET,UPSC,NDA.NTSE,KVPY,OLYMPIADS)

ACHARYA VISHVENDRA

Dedicated to the complexities faced during preparation for JEE

Contents

Foreword *vii*

Preface *ix*

Acknowledgements *xi*

Prologue *xiii*

1. Introduction 1

2. The Process 20

3. Complexities 31

4. Dealing Strategies For Complexities 61

Foreword

Preparing for a competitive exam is a long itinerary.There are ups & downs during the preparation.only those students who have control over their emotions are able to crack the competitive exams.

in our country there are a lot of teachers,schools & coaching institutes for training students about information used in competitive exams,but nobody pays attention to the emotions of a student while he prepare for competitive exam.

This book is an effort to train students on managing their negative emotions which they feel during their preparation.so that they can well manage their emotions and achieve remarkable success in academic,professional & spiritual dimensions of life.

Preface

Human beings are generally driven by emotions.whatever we do the driving force for that is our inner emotion.Managing emotions is a great skill which plays a remarkable role in success.This skill can be measured as emotional quotient(E.Q.).

This book is an effort to develop E.Q. with the help of a scientific,structured & customized process.

Acknowledgements

Thanks to life for exploring an opportunity to work on the fundamental concept of developing EMOTIONAL QUOTIENT(E.Q.)

Prologue

Cracking a competitive exam is a challenging task that require certain mental skills along with developing information processing system.This book is an effort to develop good emotional quotient so that students can crack competitive exams easily and can contribute to the vision of "Developing mind-Develop india".

CHAPTER ONE

INTRODUCTION

1.1:INTRODUCTION:

Cracking competitive exams is the most optimal way to live a quality life in our country.if you aspire to have name,fame & money then you can get all of these by cracking a competitive exam like**(JEE,NEET,CUET,UPSC,NDA,NTSE,KVPY,ICAR,JET,SSC ETC.)**

Cracking a competitive exam requires a well developed information processing system like a computer system.but we have emotions which often interfere with our working.

hence the major concern in cracking any competitive exam is managing the negative emotions like fear,anxiety,stress,depression,lack of concentration ec. which usually occurs when we prepare for a competitive exam.

This book deals with the negative emotions & the strategies to face them by developing emotional quotient gradually by working on a scientific,structured & customized process.

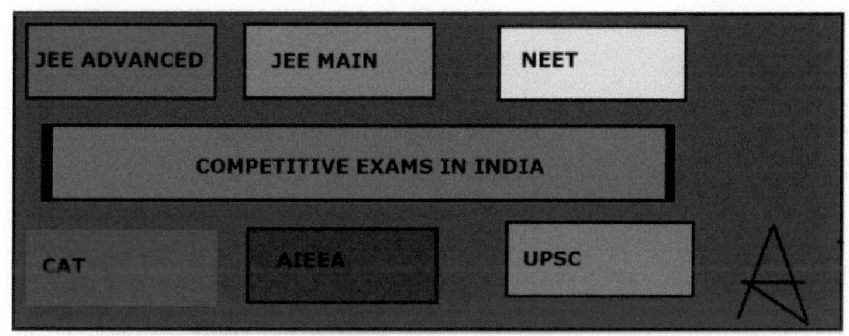

FIG. 1.1: COMPETITIVE EXAMS IN INDIA

1.2:WHAT IS EMOTIONAL QUOTIENT?

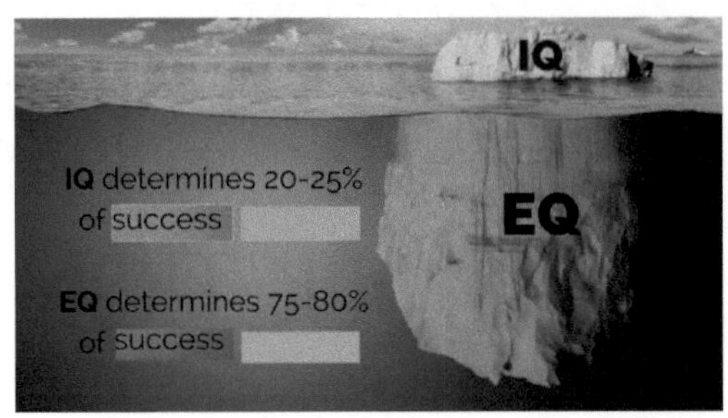

FIG. 1.2: EMOTIONAL QUOTIENT

Emotional Quotient (EQ) is the ability to observe, manage, and optimally use emotions for being successful in life.Average humans are generally driven by emotions.

They do something under the influence of their emotions only.But if we think beyond survival then emotions may be the reasons of sufferings & non productivity.

Hence to achieve above average in life we must have a control over our emotions.This power to control our own emotions is called the emotional quotient.

1.2.1: FACTORS FOR DETERMINING E.Q. ?

The 5 factors for determining E.Q. are:

1.2.1.1: INTERPERSONAL SKILLS:

FIG. 1.3: INTERPERSONAL SKILLS

Interpersonal skills are concerned with how you behave with other students & teachers.some of the key interpersonal skills for cracking competitive exams are:

(1) GOOD LISTENING HABIT: Good listening ensures.that you give importance to emotions of other students & teachers.it sends a positive non-verbal message to the other students & teachers & motivates them to be comfortable with you.some benifits of good listening are:

1.Good listening ensures better emotional relationships with others students & teachers

2.Good listening ensures analysing the message of others students & teachers

3.Good listening ensures better decision making to use the experience of others students & teachers

4.Good listening ensures positive environment for sharing experience with others students & teachers

5.Good listening ensures that others students & teachers are stimulated for better communication.

FIG. 1.4: GOOD LISTENING HABIT

(2) TAKING INITIATIVE: During your preparation of competitive exams,sometimes its better to take initiative for better learning & performance.

suppose you think a new solution to a question which is easier & quick so you should take the initiative so that ou can learn a better method.

cracking a competitive exam is based on hybrid of smart & hard working.these easy methods can help you a lot in scoring better than others.

it may seems to follow a standard method for comfortable working but taking initiative for using a new solution may leads to better & quick solutions.

FIG. 1.5: TAKING INITIATIVE:

(3) GOOD VERBAL COMMUNICATION WITH OTHER STUDENTS & TEACHERS:you may not be best at everything.

so you should consult other students & teachers for the topics in which you are not good.but that requires a good verbal interaction.

you should know how to speak with others so that they will share their knowledge with you.it saves your time & efforts and you can strengthen your topics with lesser efforts.

FIG. 1.6: GOOD VERBAL COMMUNICATION WITH OTHER STUDENTS & TEACHERS:

(4) FLEXIBLE MINDSET:you should be flexible to adapt to the changes.Everything is changing.if you are not capable to adapt with the changes,you will just struggle with your rigid mentality,

suppose you see a new type of question or a new concept relevant to youe exam.generally students are unable to adapt with the new concept rather they becomes anxious & frustrated when trying to solve that question because this question requires them to work beyond their comfort zone & usually they are unable to answer it quickly as its a new question.

so you must have a flexible mentality so that you can chnage your mentality from performer to learner whenever required.

FIG. 1.7: FLEXIBLE MINDSET

(5) WORK FOR THE WHOLE INFORMATION PROCESSING SYSTEM:

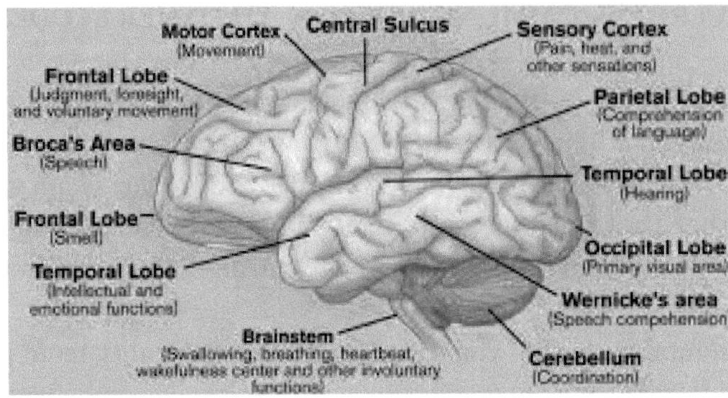

FIG. 1.8: STRUCTURE OF THE BRAIN

Our brain has different parts which all have distinct roles.we should work for developingthe whole processing system and try to get output instead of focusing only on some functions.

some students have a better memory than others,whereas some may have better analytical skills.but finding answer of a question requires all skills like analytical skills,calculations,memorization skills,creative thinking skills etc.

hence you should work for developing average skills in different functions rather than working only on 1 skill.

for example a successful student who cracks a competitive exam has developed average skills of analysis,problem solving,memorization,creative thinking etc.where as if another student has above average memorisation skills but below average analytical skills then he will generally perform lower than the first student.

Hence cracking a competitive exam requires harmonious development of mental skills rather than one specific skill.

FIG. 1.9: HARMONIOUS DEVELOPMENT

(6) ACCEPT CRITICISM:

Accept criticism with a strong mentality.think carefully & use it for your benifit.its better to have a critic because he can help you in self improvement.

FIG. 1.10: ACCEPT CRITICISM

(a)TAKE IT POSITIVELY:

FIG. 1.11: TAKE IT POSITIVELY

Take criticism positively & don't react.learn to achieve a silent state of mind under criticism. Take a deep breath & analyse your criticism.list out the points where you can improve

(b)ASK FOR ELABORATIVE ANALYSIS:

Ask your critics for elaborative analysis.What,why & how things need needs to be improved? Constructive criticism can help you to improve and perform better in competitive exams.

FIG. 1.12: ELABORATIVE ANALYSIS

1.2.2: SELF AWARENESS:

Humans have multiple faces.we are considerably different in front of society than what we are actually.so we must be aware about our mask & real face.

The problem arise when we start acting with ourself.This creates splitted personality and we feel that we ourself are divided into opposite things.

Studying is a complex & painful process initially.so students generally don't like to study but they pretend before others that we like to study.

This creates dual personality & most of the time of the students is wasted in pretending to others that they are studying rather than actually studying.

But when they don't perform in exam,they blame it on situations,time & other external factors.but they don't realise that they didn't study effectively and just acted to study.For cracking a competitive exam a student must be focused on studies rather than acting.

so a student must be aware about his reality and use his time & energy within the limits of their self awareness rather than acting to study.

FIG. 1.13: SELF AWARENESS:

1.2.3: EMPATHY:

It is the ability to know the feelings of others. generally students are surrounded by fellow students & teachers.its necessary to have empathy so that they interact with others in a constructive way,understanding their feelings and emotions & make best use of their experience.

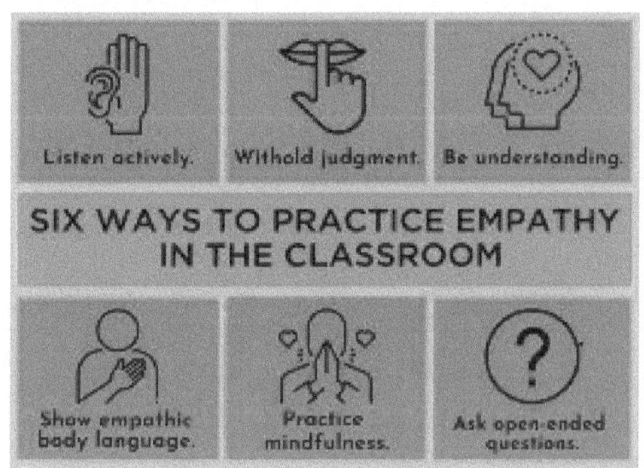

FIG. 1.14: EMPATHY

1.2.4: SELF REGULATION:

Preparing for a competitive exam is a complex process.you have to go through an emotional state of mind which will try to deviate you & confuse you in illusions.

Managing these emotions is extremly important to successfully crack the competitive exam.These emotions can be managed by learning self regulations.

FIG. 1.15: SELF REGULATION

SOME STRATEGIES FOR SELF REGULATION:

1.2.4.1: FOCUS ON PRESENT:

FIG. 1.16: FOCUS ON PRESENT

Most of the time students are either thinking about future or day dreaming about past.For effective learning its necessary to be focused at present.so develop the habit to focus on present.

1.2.4.2: LEARN IN STEPS

FIG. 1.17: LEARN IN STEPS

Any topic is composed of subtopics which are further composed of information.You can't learnthe entire topic or subtopic at a single instant.

Rather you need to work on each information which is so small that your MIND-BRAIN SYSTEM can process it.so for effective learning you should break information in so small steps which you can process effectively.

1.2.4.3: LEARN TO MANAGE EMOTIONS:

FIG. 1.18: LEARN TO MANAGE EMOTIONS

while preparing for a competitive exam you will mentally go through a complex emotional state.Managing the negative emotions is the key to success in cracking competitive exams as negative emotions interfere with your ability to perform in competitive exams.

1.2.4.4: HAVE A SILENT MIND:

FIG. 1.19: MEDITATION FOR SILENT MIND

Silent mind is the pre requisite of optimal performance.so if you aspire to have an optimal performance then have a silent mind.you can learn meditation for a silent mind.

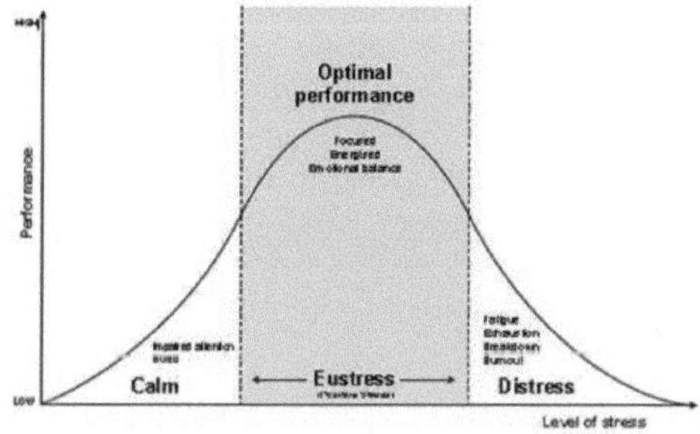

FIG. 1.20: OPTIMAL PERFORMANCE

1.2.4.5: TAKE FEEDBACK FROM OTHERS:

Take feedback from other students & teachers to know their point of view.it helps you to stay cool & calm during external feedback.its very important to check how you respond to the external feedback.if you are easily provoked and gets excited then you will face problem while performing under pressure.

FIG. 1.21: TAKE FEEDBACK FROM OTHERS

1.2.5: SELF MOTIVATION:

FIG. 1.22: SELF MOTIVATION

Self-motivation is a key trait for optimal performance in competitive exams.Its a well established fact that during odd times,nobody cares for you.you have to bear the brunt of odd time alone.and at that time self motivation plays the crucial role.

if you are not self motivated then you will break yourself during odds whereas if you are self motivated during odds you can break the records.

But how to be self-motivated? How to motivate yourself for being better? What should you do to motivate yourself?All these answers lies within you. you have to face problems head-on.once you have realized that solutions to all our problems is within ourself,you will leave dependency on others & will stay self motivated.

Stop being dependent on other people.analyse your problem & start working on them rather than expecting others to help you out.Nobody will help you if you are weak.so stand up for your purpose and fight for your aspirations.

You are the only one that can help you during odd times.You have to work on yourself. You have to optimise your mind and body for optimal results.

The source of motivation lies within us hence be self dependent,don't expect others to help you out & fight with situations to get what you aspire for.

1.2.6:WHY GOOD EQ IS NECESSARY?

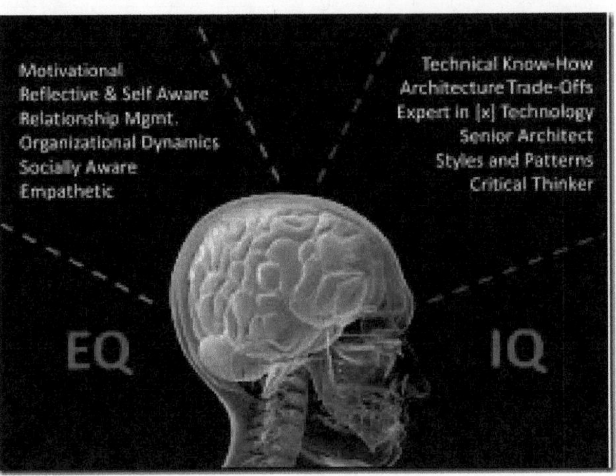

FIG. 1.23: COMPETITIVE EXAMS IN INDIA

Emotionally intelligent leaders create safer working environments in which employees thrive. Employees openly communicate, share ideas, and take risks in such environments. This leads to the building of organizations that have collaborative working ingrained in their culture.

FIG. 1.24: EMOTIONAL INTELLIGENCE

Emotionally intelligent students have what it takes to make them crack the competitive exam with a good rank. They works recursively to get the best performance out of them.They updates their plans & strategies for better results, They observe & analyse their emotions very well & plan accordingly so that they can well manage their emotions and have best performance as per their capabilities.

Students with high EQ are so successful because they manage their emotional conflicts well and are highly focused on results.

FIG. 1.25: EMOTIONALLY INTELLIGENT STUDENT

While emotional conflicts between various emotions is very common while you prepare for competitive exam.its very common to have anxiety,stress,depression,confusion,mental blockage etc.but these things can be well managed by continuous working.

FIG. 1.26: EMOTIONAL CONFLICTS

With practice you can learn how to manage your emotions.Emotional conflicts within a student are responsible for poor performance in exams.hence emotional conflicts should be well managed.

FIG. 1.27: MANAGE YOUR EMOTIONS FOR BETTER PERFORMANCE

The biggest reason for their emotional conflict in students is that they are not emotionally intelligent.They gets frustrated over small issues.while emotionally intelligent students are neutral to emotions. This leads to optimal performance in exams.

FIG. 1.28: FRUSTRATED STUDENT

As explained earlier there is a need of working as a system for harmonious working of the "MIND-BRAIN SYSTEM" for better results. working with just 1 part of the "MIND-BRAIN SYSTEM" may sound comfortable but it can't create results.

Hence having emotional intelligence and a good emotional quotient is necessary for better performance in competitive exams.

FIG. 1.29: GOOD E.Q.IS NECESSARY FOR OPTIMAL PERFORMANCE

CHAPTER TWO

THE PROCESS

2.1:INTRODUCTION:

Emotional intelligence or high emotional quotient(E.Q.) can be developed with a scientific,structured & customized process as given below-

FIG. 2.1:THE PROCESS

Lets start with the process of developing E.Q. since we are aspiring to crack competitive exam which deals with our ability to solve M.C.Q.'S, so our E.Q. should be in the plane of cracking competitive exam by learning to solve M.C.Q.S.

2.2: LEARNING THE PROCESS:

when you start learning to solve a question then your "**mind-brain system**" will follow a pattern.you will feel emotional conflicts while trying to get answer from the question.so just observe the pattern and learn to cope up with the pattern to learn emotional intelligence for competitive exams.

LEARNING THE PROCESS

FIG. 2.2: LEARNING THE PROCESS

2.2.1:LET'S START:

FIG. 2.3: LET'S START

just start solving M.C.Q.'S & observe your emotions with an unbiased & silent mind.your emotion will folllow a pattern.observe this pattern & optimise it for optimal results.

FIG. 2.4: MCQ PATTERN

2.2.2:THE PATTERN OF EMOTIONS:

FIG. 2.5: THE PATTERN OF EMOTIONS

The complete emotional pattern while solving M.C.Q. is:

1. STATE OF UNSTABLE THOUGHTS:

Normally the "**MIND-BRAIN SYSTEM**" of students is busy either in future or past.and its a normal situation.but when we need to solve a question we need to access a particular information and that is quite a complex task.

Thats why its so hard to get an answer while so easy to ask a question.initially students have to fight with there past habits to change their focus from past or future to present which is a very painful process because by default mind has the nature of being free.

when we assign the task to find a specific information it feels like being a slave & it tries its best to escape from being slave.while this property of mind is a boon to access higher dimensions of life but it is a bane for materialistic dimensions.As in materialistic dimensions there are manipulations and slavery of enjoyments.

This wandering mind is the conscious mind which changes to subconscious & finally unconscious mind which is reflected in changing thought pattern of the "**MIND-BRAIN SYSTEMS**".

FIG. 2.6: UNSTABLE THOUGHTS

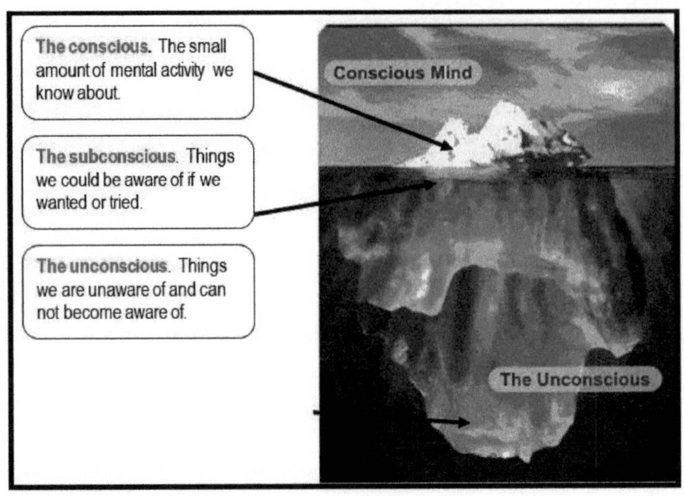

FIG. 2.7: HUMAN MINDS AS PER SIGMUN FREUD THEORY

FIG. 2.8: A FRUSTRATED STUDENT DUE TO UNSTABLE THOUGHTS

2. STATE OF STABLE THOUGHTS:

Initially students are not able to get access to the desired information but with practice gradually a state of stable thoughts arise and students can comfortably get access to the desired information as and when needed.

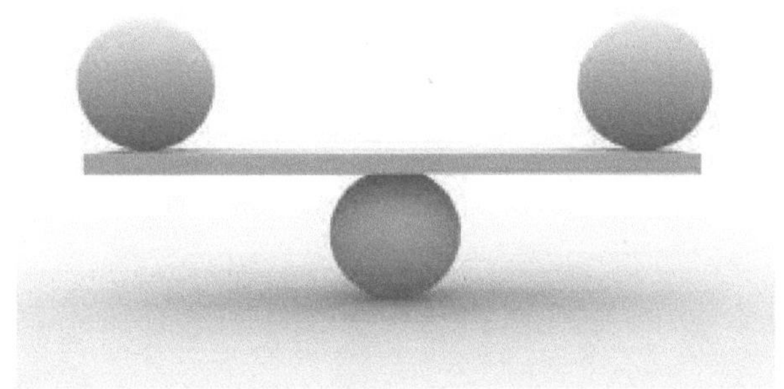

FIG. 2.9: STABLE THOUGHTS

FIG. 2.10: A COMFORTABLE STUDENT DUE TO STABLE THOUGHTS

3. ANALYSIS OF THE QUESTION:

when we have stable thoughts the next task is to analyse the question.Analysis is done to fetch the desired information for solving the question.The analysis consists of asking ourself that this question is from:

1.Which chapter?

2.Which topic?
3.which subtopic?
4.Which formulas ?

FIG. 2.11: ANALYSIS OF THE QUESTION

4. INFORMATION RETRIEVAL:

Studying is a process of information storage in your long term memory.But you can't access long term memory directly.you have to go through a pattern of sensory memory then short term memory & at last the long term memeory.This process is the key factor in deciding your success in competitive exam as most of the students are unable to transfer information to long term memory.

Hence master the process of information transfer to the long term memory.after information storage its also necessary to backtrack the information.back tracking ensures that a neural pathway is created to transfer information from sensory to long term memory & vice versa.

process each information in the same pattern and develop a well structured information processing system within your "MIND-BRAIN SYSTEM".

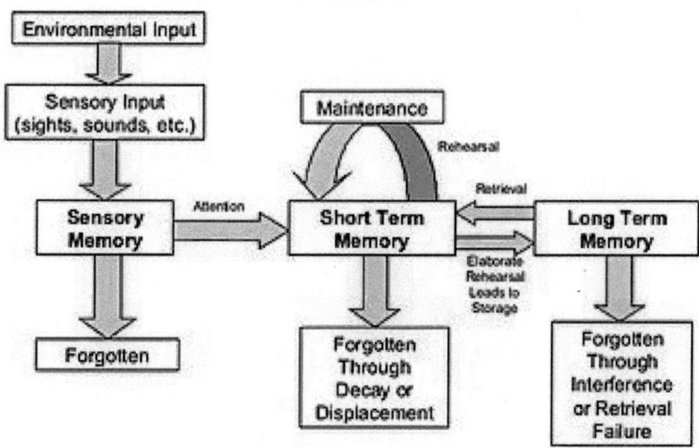

FIG. 2.12: INFORMATION PROCESSING MODEL IN HUMAN MIND-BRAIN SYSTEM

1.sensory memory: When you study a book information reaches to the sensory memory through your senses,mostly eyes & ears.

2.Short term memory: After sensory memory your mind-brain system starts mind mapping in which the sensory memory is mapped with temporary memory/short term memory.

3.Long term memory: After mapping with short term memory,information gets mapped with long term memory/ permanent memory.

As shown in the figure the information processing in human "MIND-BRAIN SYSTEM" conists of storing & retrieving memory from sensory to long term & from long term to sensory memory.

After analysis the task is to fetch desired information so that you can solve the question.

Hence when you study,use this pattern.Dont just study as a formality,make sure that whatever you study its able to reach your log term memory.have a testing of yourself by retrieving the information.

for example:suppose you are studying first equation of motion which is v=u+at

so you should procee like this:

1.step-1:read "first equation of motion",try to map it with temporary/short term memory,this is a natural process.you just focus on "first equation of motion".your short term memory will try to connect this information.try to feel each word of "first equation of motion" and create a mental map.

you can think that our space is 3 Dimensional so it can be explained by 3 equations.This is just a memory trick to create a mind map between sensory & temporary memory.once when you have created a map between sensory & temporary memory,it's necessary to create a map between temporary and permanent memory.

permanent memory is accessed without any active effort or it is automatic,but transferring information from temporary memory/short term memory to permanent memory/long term memory is a challenging task.repeat information transfer 3 times & more in multiples of 3 if needed.

test yourself for retrieving memory till you are able to retrieve information perfectly.

FIG. 2.13: MEMORY RETRIEVAL

5. CRITICAL THINKING: Information is not sufficient to solve a question.you need to have the skills of critical thinking.Any question uses 2 things information & process.suppose you are given a question like:

A particle is moving along x axis with a velocity 10m/sec.if it has a constant accelration of 2m/sec2.then find the velocity of particle at t=5 sec.

ask yourself

1.what is relation between velocity and acceleration?(The thinking process)

2.search for for relevant information;the information that you will get is v=u+at(information retrieval from permanent memory)

3.calculate v=u+at;v=10+(2*5)=10+10=20(the calculation process)

Solving Any question requires information & process. The process involves critical thinking,calculating etc.critical thinking is the multistep process to fetch desired information from permanent memory as and when needed.

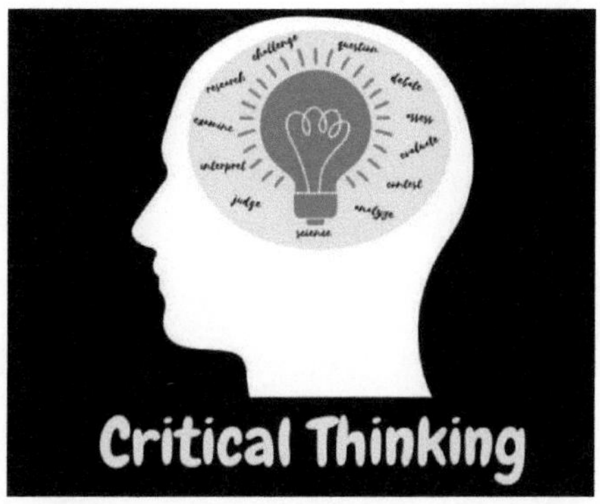

FIG. 2.14: CRITICAL THINKING

6.CALCULATIONS:

After critical thinking the next step is calculation.this is an important process and should be performed with unbroken focus.calculation mistakes can ruin the entire process and may end up in wrong option which can lead to negative marking.

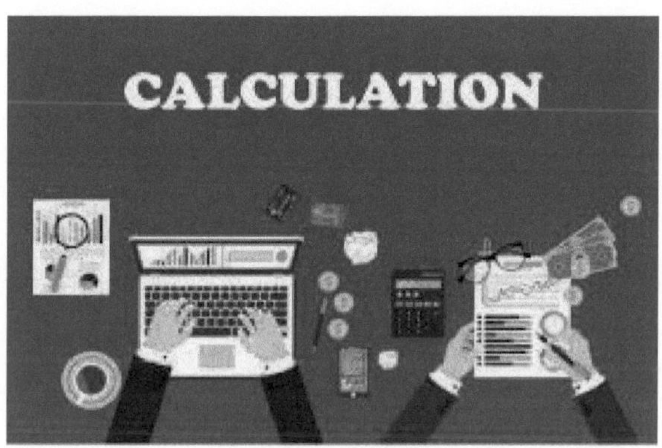

FIG. 2.15: CALCULATIONS

7.MARKING THE ANSWER:

The last but not the least step is marking answers.This step is also extremly imporatnt as iot is the final step so make sure that you mark the correct answer correctly.

FIG. 2.16: MARKING THE ANSWER

CHAPTER THREE

COMPLEXITIES

3.1:INTRODUCTION:

Developing E.Q. is a complex and time consuming process.You can't develop your E.Q. instantly.so you have to design a well structured time limit to ensure developement of effective emotional quotient.

According to Phillippa Lally; a health psychology researcher at University College London, a new habit usually takes a little more than 2 months — 66 days to be exact — and as much as 254 days until it's fully formed.

The study was based on the behavior of 96 participants who were asked to pick a habit and practice it for 12 weeks. The participants reported to the researcher how automatic their new behavior felt over time. Undoubtedly, the results varied drastically from one person to another leading the researcher to claim that automaticity (i.e how automatic the new behavior felt over time) takes between three to twelve times longer than 21 days.

(source:https://medium.com/swlh/21-day-habit-timeline-how-to-form-a-habit-in-21-days-day-by-day-92298446bf6b)

The process of developing your E.Q. is a complex process.during the process you will feel complexities which are discussed in the next section

FIG. 3.1: COMPLEXITIES

3.2:SOME COMPLEXITIES:

3.2.1:FEAR:

Students are generally afraid of new things.if a student has not learnt the information processing in "**MIND-BRAIN SYSTEM**",

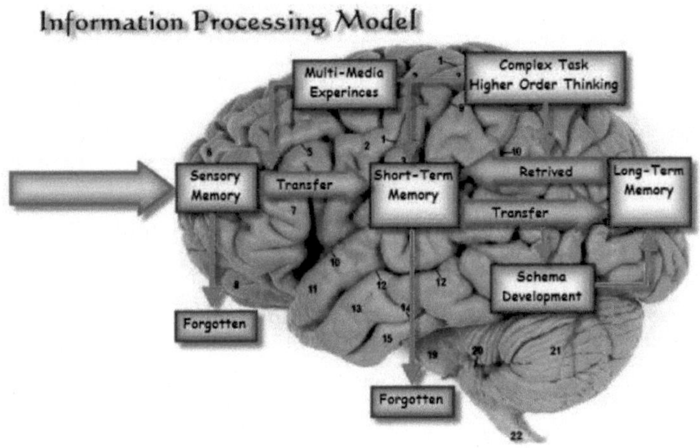

FIG. 3.2: INFORMATION PROCESSING IN "MIND-BRAIN SYSTEM"

then initially he will be afraid.you might have seen that people are generally afraid of questions because answering a question requires specific information & process.Most of the times, we are trapped in random & automatic thoughts but when we try to access specific information and process.we feel negative emotions the first of which is a feeling of fear.

FIG. 3.3: FEAR

FIG. 3.4: FEAR

The feeling of fear can be related to accessing higher energy centres/chakra in human body. It is beleived that human body itself is the entire universe.it has 114 energy centres,out of which 112 energy centres lies in body and 2 outside the body.out of these 112 energy centres there are 7 main centres/chakras.The basic chakra is the muladhar/root chakra.when your consciousness rises above the muladhar chakra then you feel negative emotions like fear,anxiety,depression,hurry,inability to focus,jealousy etc.

FIG. 3.5: 7 MAIN ENERGY CENTRES/CHAKRAS IN HUMAN BODY

FIG. 3.6: HIGHER DIMENSIONS OF CONSCIOUSNESS

FIG. 3.7: ILLUSIONS

As it is said that nature has trapped our minds in maya & secrets of creation lies in accessing higher dimensions of consciousness.you might have heard of sage vishwamitra who was meditating & lord indra tried to make him loose his path using rambha & menka.

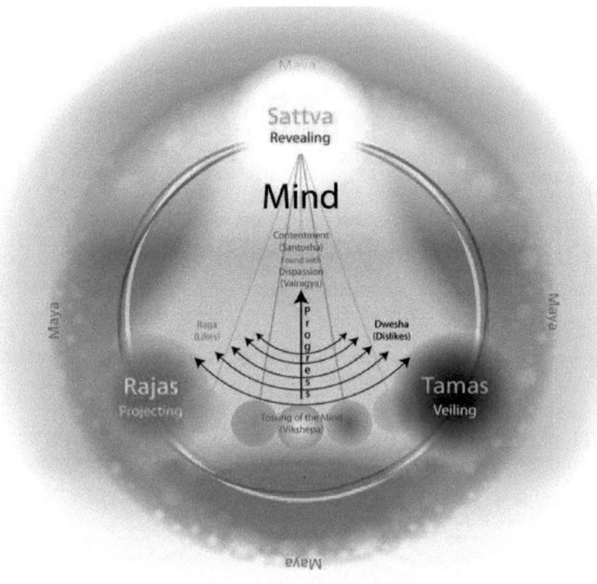

FIG. 3.8: MAYA

so nature will test you for your mental strength when you will try to access higher dimensions of consciousness.

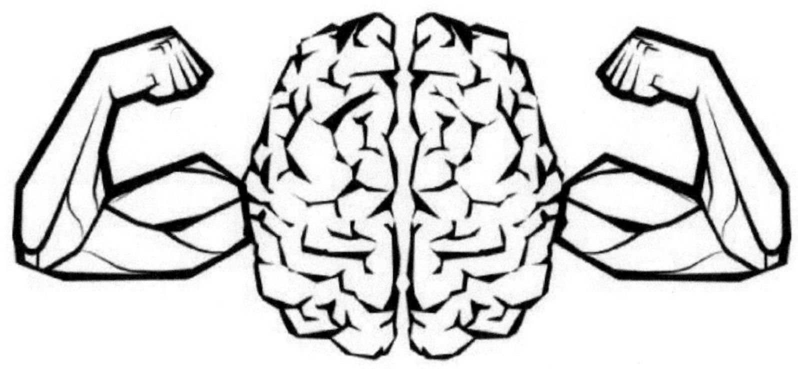

FIG. 3.9: MENTAL STRENGTH

3.2.2:HURRY:

FIG. 3.10: HURRY

Solving a question demands multitasking.you have to analyse,retain information,calculate,manage emotions at the same time.Thats why we feel a different version of ourself when we solve a question.This multitasking has to be well managed & switching between differetnt tasks have to be separtaed by optimal time gap so that we are able to perform multitasking effectively.

generally interuption of various processes occurs which leads to loss in focus.

FIG. 3.11: INTERRUPTION

FIG. 3.12: MULTITASKING CAN LEAD TO LOWER PERFORMANCE

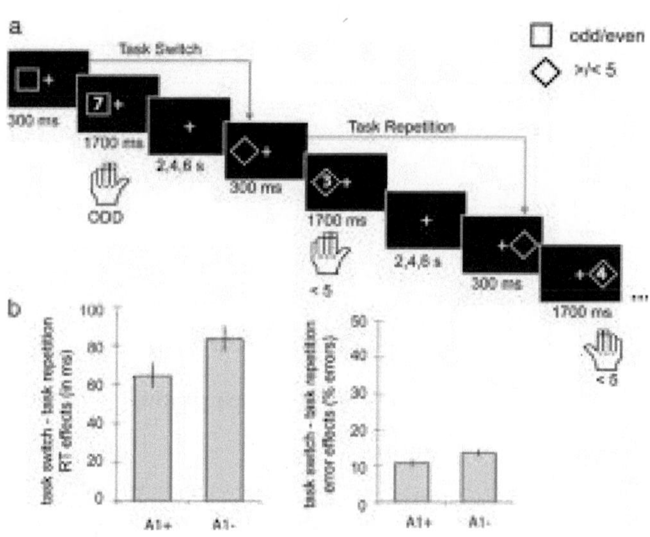

FIG. 3.13: TIME GAP BETWEEN MULTITASK

But sometimes time space allocated for switching between different tasks is less than optimal time space .This leads to hurry sickness. It's an emotional stste of anxiety.it looks like you have lost control over everything. Sometimes students when trying to solve a problem suffers from hurry.they feel like they have lost cntrol over everything.they feel a mental state of anxiety,low self esteem & mental fatigue.

FIG. 3.14: ANXIOUS STUDENT

3.2.3: INABILITY TO FOCUS:

FIG. 3.15: INABILITY TO FOCUS

It's a phenomenon when a student is unable to focus on his study and constantly feels distractions. The phenomenon of inability to focus can be analysed in terms of 3 events:

1.STRUGGLING TO CONCENTRATE:

FIG. 3.16: STRUGGLING TO CONCENTRATE

2. CYNICISM: Cynicism is a defence mechanism to cope up with our inefiiciency. It's typically triggered when a good student see a new concept or question and instead of solving the question he is hurt as it will decline his image in front of other students.

FIG. 3.17: CYNICISM

3.INEFFICIENT LEARNING:

Students are unable to learn effectively.their performance is very poor.They are not able to regenertae the concpt that they learnt,when they appear in exam.They forget concept completly or partly but in each case their performance is not upto the mark & they are not able to crack the competitive exam.

FIG. 3.18: INEFFICIENT LEARNING

3.2.4: STUDY BURNOUTS?

Study burnouts refers to the emotional state when you don't feel like studying.you will feel irritation,reflective mind.you will find repulsion from studies.The intensity of these symptoms varies from student to student. It is related to the ability of students to perform under pressure. it is a common misconception that burnout is a result of studying too hard for too long.Its infact the inability to manage your emotions under pressure like during competitive exam. Some symptoms of study burnouts are:

1.LOW SELF CONFIDENCE:

Students feel being tired,inactive & incapable of working.Their brainwave frequency drops very low to delta reason as an impact of which they feel low self confidence.They are unable to manage their emotions and feel like a looser

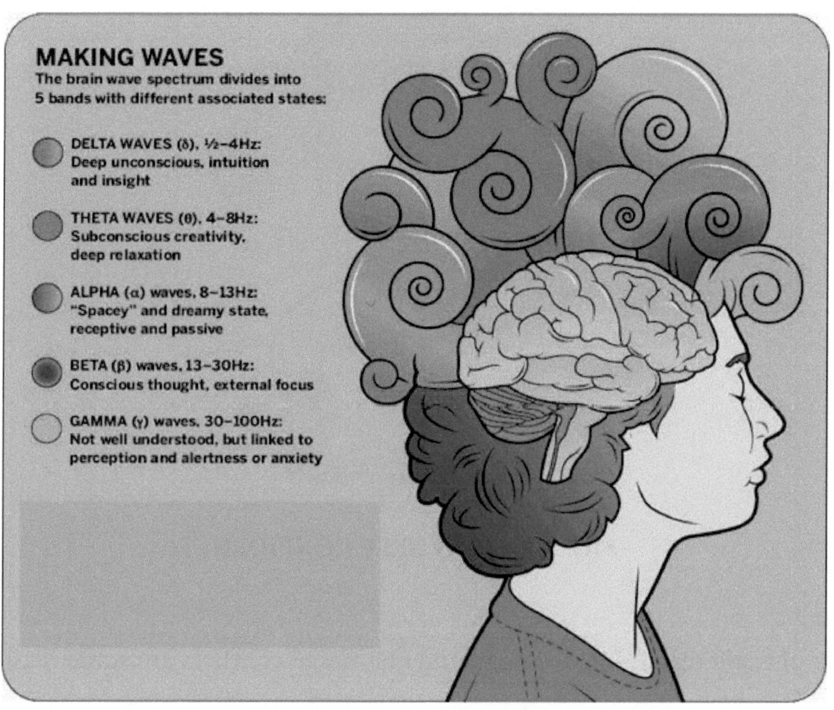

Enter Caption

FIG. 3.19: LOW SELF CONFIDENCE

2.MENTAL FATIGUE:
Too much stress, fear of exam result,sleeplessness, and emotional conflicts are some reasons of mental fatigue.

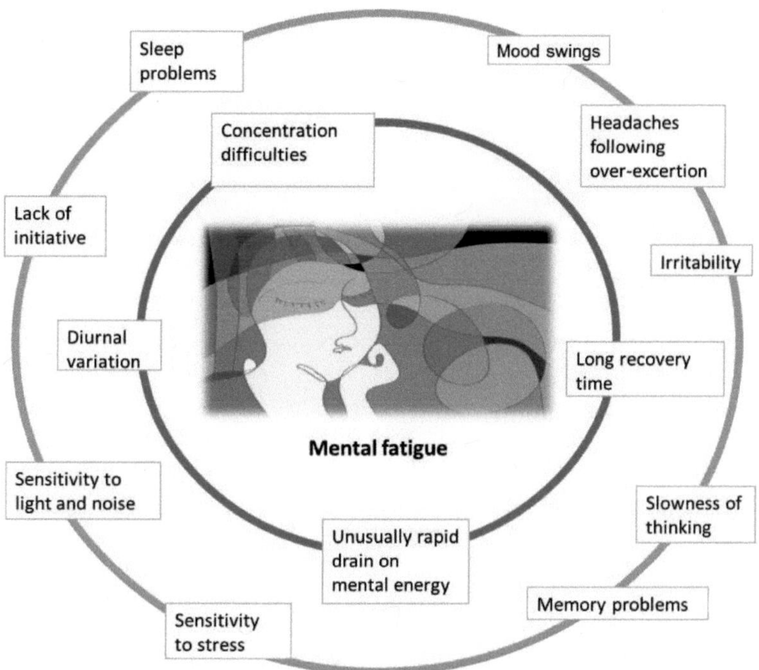

FIG. 3.20: MENTAL FATIGUE

3.ABRUPT DECLINATION IN PERFORMANCE:

The performance of student drops abruptly.his marks and ranks are severly affected.in some cases student from top can become student from bottom.

FIG. 3.21: ABRUPT DECLINATION IN PERFORMANCE

3.2.5:ANXIETY:

FIG. 3.22: ANXIETY

Anxiety is a mental state which is often perceived as a state of confusion,fear,restlessness.some of the symptoms of anxiety are:

1.MENTAL SYMPTOMS: Some of the mental symptoms of anxiety are:

Repetitive Thoughts,Negative Self-Talk,Disorientation,Thoughts Of Dying,Thoughts Of Going Crazy Thoughts Of Being Out Of Control,Persistent Worries,Difficulty Concentrating,Frightening Images

2.PHYSICAL SYMPTOMS: Some of the physical symptoms of anxiety are:

Trembling,Muscle Tension,Shortness Of Breath,Accelerated Heart Rate,Heart Palpitations,Sweating,Dizziness,Dry Mouth,Easily Startled,Fatigue,Frequent Urination,Trouble Swallowing,Reduced Appetite/Nausea/Diarrhea

3.PERSONALITY SYMPTOMS: Some of the personality symptoms of anxiety are:

Avoidance,Disturbed Sleep,Not Attending Classes,Procrastination,Increased Alcohol Use,Increased Caffeine Use,Distractibility,Restlessness

FIG. 3.23: ANXIETY SYMPTOMS

FIG. 3.24: ANXIETY SYMPTOMS

3.2.5: WEAK PROBLEM SOLVING SKILLS:

The students preparing for competitive exams have to transform from passive listeners or information receivers to active problem solvers.It shifts the focus of classroom teaching from teaching to learning. It enables the students to learn how to apply the information learnt by solving the questions.

FIG. 3.25: WEAK PROBLEM SOLVING SKILLS

FIG. 3.26: PROBLEM SOLVING SKILLS

FIG. 3.27: PROBLEM SOLVING SKILLS

FIG. 3.28: PROBLEM SOLVING SKILLS

Generally classroom teaching is monotonous & boring and after sometime genrally students loose their interest in the class.thats why most of the students fails in competitive exams because cracking a competitive exam requires active learning & problem solving skills.students have poor problem solving skills thats why most of them fails in competitive exams.

FIG. 3.29: EMOTIONAL PATTERN OF A STUDENT DURING SUCCESSIVE SCHOOLING

FIG. 3.30: STUDENT FEELING BOREDOM IN CLASS

problem-solving involves information processing,cognitive learning,emotional stability etc.in short problem solving skill is a part of your personality not some formula or trick.you have to develop problem solving with a continuous & gradual process.

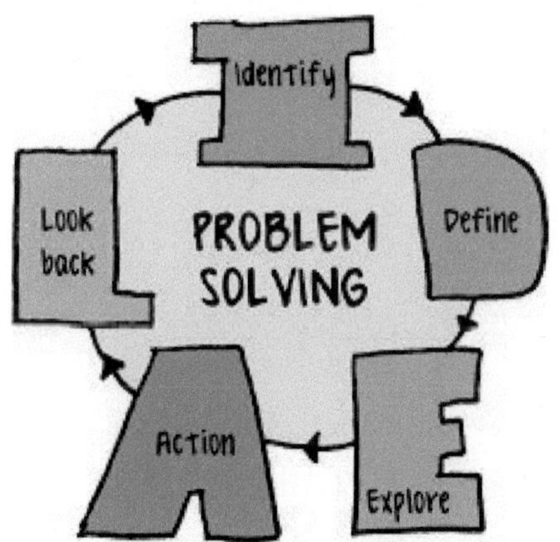

FIG. 3.31: HUMAN CHAKRA SYSTEM

Problem solving skills can be defined with three key traits:

1.Problem-solving is an object-oriented working:

Problem solving is an object oriented working where you start wih the vision to find answer

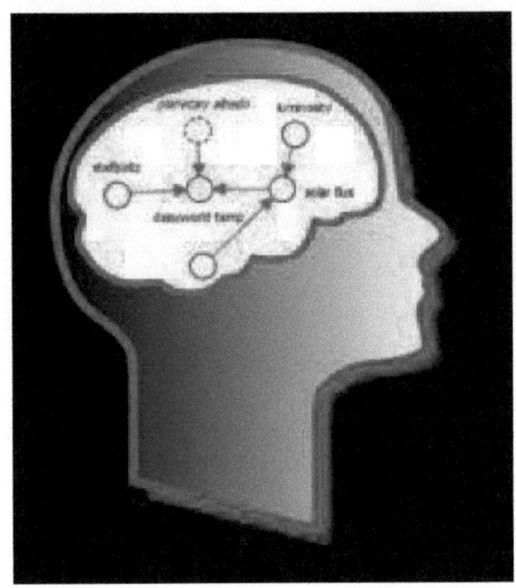

FIG. 3.32: HUMAN CHAKRA SYSTEM

2. Problem solving is a process :

it involves the manipulation of knowledge,use of information processing,decision making,emotional balance and ability to perform under stress.

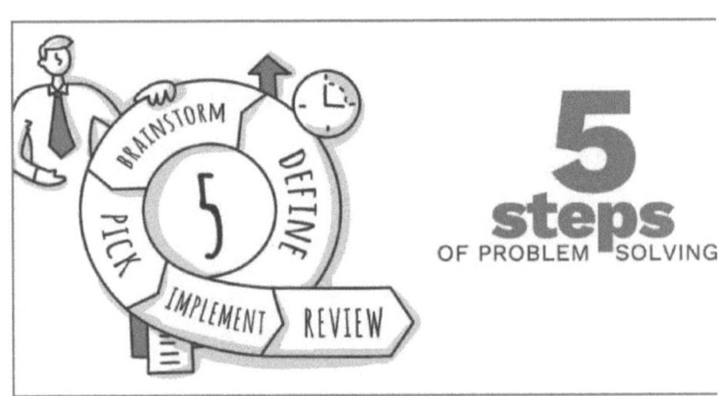

FIG. 3.33: HUMAN CHAKRA SYSTEM

3. Problem-solving is a habit & related with cognitive learning:

its not an instantaneous process.you have to develop problem solving skills by continuous working ,analysis & improvements.

FIG. 3.34: HUMAN CHAKRA SYSTEM

FIG. 3.35: COMPLEXITIES

3.2.6:WEAK ANALYTICAL SKILLS:

Weak analytical skills are reflected in some of the following cognitive process of students.for example:

1.Negative thinking:

Negative thinking like "i can't solve this question","this chapter is too tough" "i don't have the potential to crack this exam" dissipates enthusiam & acive working states leading to poor performance in exam.

FIG. 3.36: NEGATIVE THINKING

2.Being judgemental:

A judgmental student think that he knows everything.He too quickly arrive at conclusion.He often judge other students & teachers.Criticise them unnecessarily & act like a boss.but it shifts his focus from working on his targets to criticising others.

Such students generally have have three common traits:

1.They enforce their evaluation system on others

2.They are extremly critical

3.They have poor social behaviour

FIG. 3.37: NEGATIVE THINKING

3.Making assumptions:

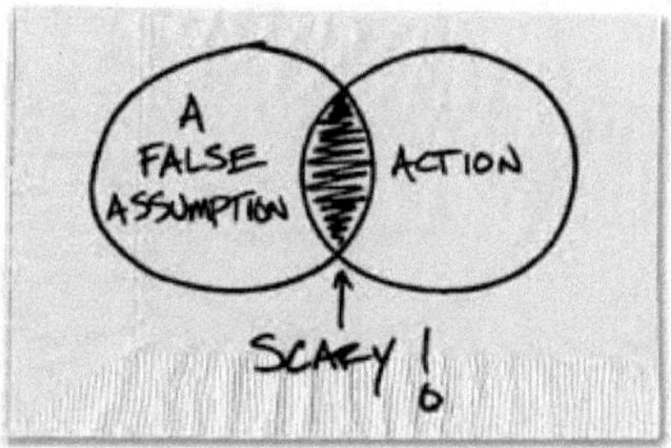

FIG. 3.38: NEGATIVE THINKING

4.Losing interest in the issue:

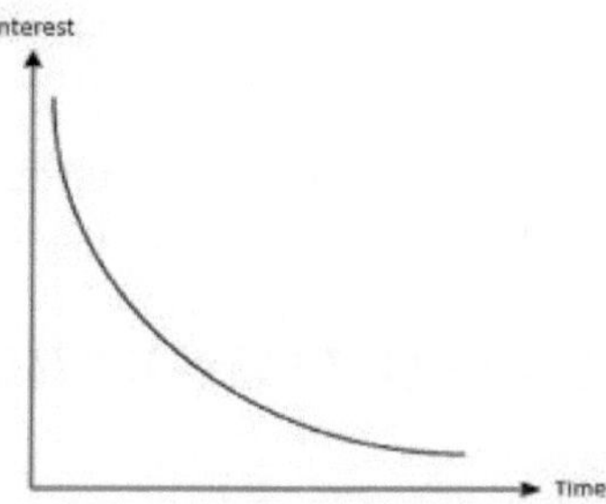

FIG. 3.39: NEGATIVE THINKING

5.Using inaccurate information:

FIG. 3.40: NEGATIVE THINKING

6.Biased thinking:

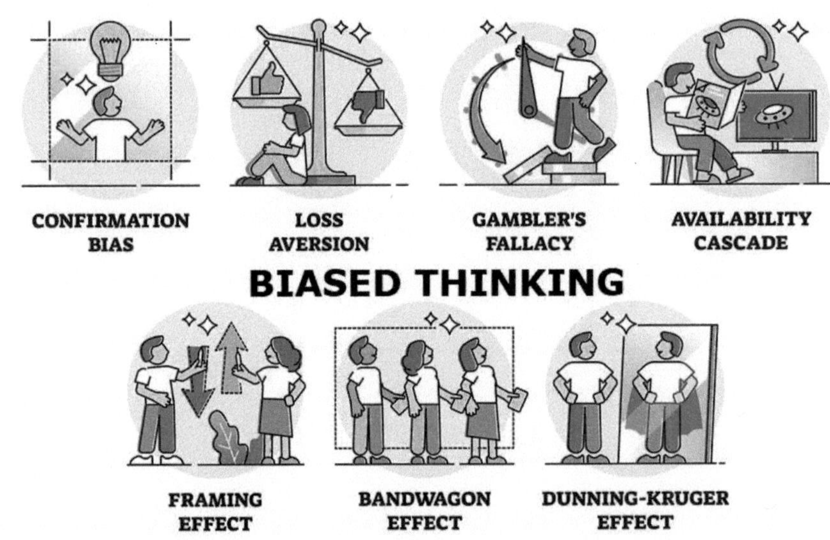

FIG. 3.41: NEGATIVE THINKING

3.2.7: WEAK PERFORMANCE :

Most of the stuents are afraid of exam which is called the exam phobia.They are unable to retain their learning during exam.

FIG. 3.43: NEGATIVE THINKING

Generally students struggles a lot during exam and are unable to perform optimally.This is because they are not able to get adapted to exam environment and during exam they are not able to perform optimally.

FIG. 3.44: NEGATIVE THINKING

There is an abrupt decrease in performance due to unadaptive mentality

FIG. 3.45: ABRUPT DECLINATION IN PERFORMANCE

FIG. 3.46: ABRUPT DECLINATION IN PERFORMANCE

FIG. 3.47: ABRUPT DECLINATION IN PERFORMANCE

FIG. 3.48: ABRUPT DECLINATION IN PERFORMANCE

So these were some of the complexities that a stuent generally face when he will start developing his emotional quotient(E.Q.)lets discuss the dealing strategies for these complexities in the next chapter

CHAPTER FOUR

DEALING STRATEGIES FOR COMPLEXITIES

All these problems can be resolved by having a silent & powerful mind system.refer to the book"DEVELOPING MIND-DEVELOP INDIA(OST)" & learn dealing strategies to cope up with these complexities.

This book is available online on amazon,flipcart & notion press.you can buy it online.

DEVELOPING MIND-DEVELOP INDIA

9 798887 493558

Printed by Libri Plureos GmbH in Hamburg,
Germany